Can astronauts see me?

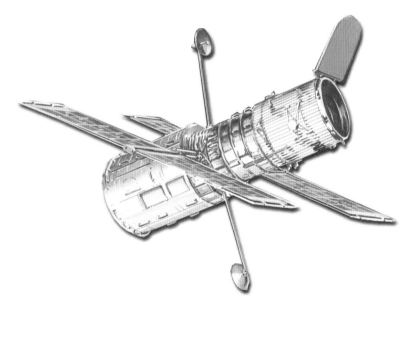

Space

Contents

2

3

What is outer space?

This is where the stars and planets are found. When it's dark, you can sometimes see some of these stars and planets. They look like twinkly dots of light in the night sky. Earth is a planet, and it's the planet on which we all live. Space and everything in it is called the Universe.

Milky Way

Planets

Comet

Spacecraft

Our Solar System

The Milky Way
On a clear night, you may see a misty, white patch in the sky. This is our galaxy, called the Milky Way. It is made up of the light from millions of stars.

Inside the Solar System
Our Solar System is in the galaxy. The Solar System is the name for all the planets, moons, and stars that move around the Sun. There are many solar systems in the Universe.

Deep in space

Nearby galaxies

? True or false

People who travel into outer space are called astronauts.

True. Astronauts have traveled in rockets to the Moon and have explored space. One day, we may all be able to travel to the Moon and visit other planets.

How big is space?

Bigger than anything you can ever imagine, and it's still growing! You can see how the Universe is getting bigger if you blow up a balloon. The Universe stretches as it gets bigger, like the balloon. Some people think that in millions of years' time, the Universe will start to shrink, like the balloon when the air is let out.

How is a star made?

A star is made when a huge cloud of gas and dust forms in space. The cloud shrinks and starts to spin and then becomes hotter and hotter. When it gets really hot, the star is born. The star then starts to shine, which is what you can see at night.

Are stars star-shaped?

Stars are ball-shaped, just like our Sun. Sometimes they look pointed if you peer at them at night. This is because the air in the sky moves around. It makes the light beams from the star shake and twinkle.

→ Grandad star

Our Sun is a star. As it grows old, it will shrivel up into a little old star called a white dwarf. One day, it will stop shining, and you won't see it anymore.

Do you know?

1. Which stars are the hottest— reds, yellows, or blues?
2. Do stars grow old?

Answers: 1. Blues. 2. Yes, they do. Stars are born, grow old, and then die.

← Dotty pictures

For thousands of years, people have imagined lines joining up groups of stars to make pictures. They gave these pictures names. One of them is called Cancer the Crab because it looks like a crab.

Are stars colored?

Stars can be lots of different colors. The color depends on how hot the star is. The hottest stars are pale blue. Yellow and orange stars are in the middle. Red stars are the coolest.

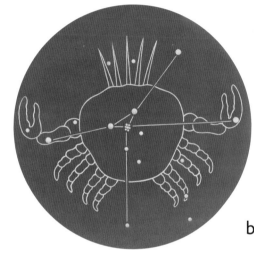

Do stars vanish?

Stars don't last forever. Stars burn for a very long time, but after a while they stop shining because they don't have enough fuel to keep on burning. Some stars fizzle out, and others explode with a huge bang. Stars that explode throw out lots of dust. Sometimes this dust clumps together to make a new star.

← Calling Earth
There are many people who believe they have seen UFOs. These are unidentified flying objects. Some people think they are alien spacecraft.

Can you see black holes?

No, they are invisible. Scientists know they are there because of what happens around them. Anything that comes near a black hole, such as gas, stars, and light, is pulled toward it. This forms a swirling disc around the black hole. Sometimes jets of gas shoot from the swirling disc into space. Scientists can see this through their telescopes.

Can we speak to beings from space?

Some scientists are listening for messages from space. They use special equipment to pick up any strange signals that might be sent by other life-forms. They haven't heard anything yet.

Where are we in space?

Planet Earth is part of a galaxy called the Milky Way. This is an enormous whirling, swirling mass of stars and planets. Our Sun and Moon are also in the Milky Way. In the middle of the galaxy is a big bulge. Scientists think this may be made up of millions of old stars.

How old is the Sun?

Very young in cosmic years! It takes one Earth year for our planet to travel around the Sun. It takes the Sun one cosmic year to go around the middle of the Milky Way. A cosmic year is 200 million Earth years. This makes the Sun about 25 years old.

Round about
The Milky Way is a spiral shape with long, trailing parts called "arms."

Do galaxies form groups?

Galaxies stick together in the same way that stars gather in galaxies. Our Milky Way galaxy is one of a group called the Local Group. This contains about 30 other galaxies.

Do you know?

1. What is the name of our galaxy?
2. What is in the middle of the Milky Way?

Answers: 1. The Milky Way. 2. A bulge containing lots of stars.

→ **Cosmic shapes**
The Milky Way galaxy is a spiral shape. But some galaxies do not have any particular shape. These are called irregular galaxies. There are also some oval-shaped galaxies, called elliptical galaxies.

elliptical galaxy

spiral galaxy

irregular galaxy

What is the Solar System?

The planets and moons, including **Earth and the Moon, go around the Sun.** There are seven other planets in our Solar System. Nearest to the Sun are the small planets, Mercury, Venus, Earth, and Mars. Then there are giant planets, called Jupiter, Saturn, Uranus, and Neptune. Farthest away is Pluto, which is very cold because it is so far from the Sun.

Neptune

Uranus

Saturn

Many moons
Earth has one Moon, which you can see at night. The other planets have their own moons. Saturn has more than 30 moons.

→ Traveling around the Sun

The word "solar" means "of the Sun." The Sun and the planets that go around it are part of the Solar System. So are all the moons and other bits of space rock.

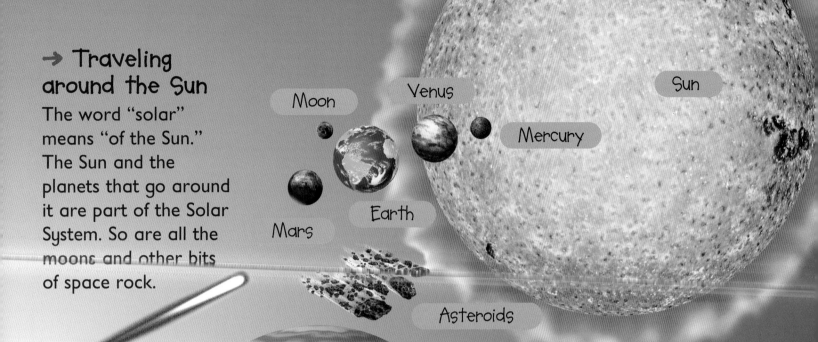

Moon

Venus

Sun

Mercury

Mars

Earth

Asteroids

Comet

Jupiter

← Orbiting

An orbit is the path something takes to go around a planet. The planet Mercury has the shortest orbit, or path, around the Sun because it doesn't have very far to go. Its orbit takes 88 days. Earth takes one year.

What else goes around in space?

Lumps of rock called asteroids and comets also orbit the Sun. Comets are made up of chunks of ice and dust. When comets come close to the Sun, the ice and dust melt and make a long trailing tail.

Can astronauts see me?

No, you would be too small for an astronaut to see. Astronauts looking down on Earth see the oceans, which look bright blue. Water makes Earth very special. If we didn't have water on our planet, nothing would be able to grow. Astronauts also see the land, which is a mixture of greens, browns, and yellows, and the white clouds.

Is the Moon made of cheese?

No, but sometimes the Moon looks like a big cheese with holes in it. These holes are called craters and were made by space rocks that crashed into the Moon. There are no winds or storms on the Moon to smooth the craters away.

← Face facts

People used to joke that there was a man in the Moon. When the Moon is full, it does look as if it has a face with eyes, a nose, and a mouth!

Why does day become night?

As well as traveling around the Sun, the Earth spins like a top! When one half of the Earth is facing the Sun, the other half is facing away. When a place on Earth faces the Sun, it is day there; when it faces away, it is night.

→ Moon change

Sometimes you can see all of the Moon, then you see only parts of it, and then sometimes you can hardly see it at all! The bright full Moon we see is when the sunlit part is facing us.

new Moon

first quarter

full Moon

15

Is Mars like Earth?

It might have been. There are huge valleys on Mars, which may once have been rivers. Some scientists believe that many years ago, it may have rained on Mars. Now Mars is a very dry and dusty planet. Like Earth, Mars has sand dunes and mountains—it even has volcanoes!

Which planet is the fastest?

Mercury is the fastest planet in the Solar System. It orbits around the Sun much faster than any of the other planets. It is named after the ancient Roman god, Mercury, who was a speedy messenger. Mercury has craters like the Moon and huge cliffs.

Mercury

↑ Birthday bonanza!

A day on the planet Mercury lasts twice as long as a year on Earth. So on Mercury, you could celebrate two birthdays every day!

? True or false

Earth is the hottest planet.

False. Venus is the hottest planet because it has a blanket of gas around it that traps the heat. Although Mercury is the planet closest to the Sun, it doesn't have a blanket of clouds to help keep the air warm.

A giant volcano on Mars

→ World of war

Mars is sometimes called the Red Planet because its rust-colored surface looks red. It is colder than Earth because it is a long way from the Sun. Mars is named after the Roman god of war.

Mars

Which planet shines?

Venus is the brightest planet in the sky. Planets shine because sunlight bounces off them. Venus is also called the morning or evening star.

Venus

Which is the giant?

Jupiter is by far the biggest planet in the Solar System. It is so enormous that you could fit all the eight other planets inside it and still have room to spare. Jupiter is also the heaviest planet.

← Pink moon
One of Neptune's moons has pink frost! The frost forms on the surface, freezes in the cold, and turns pink.

Which are blue?

The planets Uranus and Neptune both look blue. They are made up of gases. One of these gases is methane, which is blue-colored. These planets do not have a solid ground like the Earth.

Neptune

Jupiter

Saturn

Uranus

Which planet has rings?

Saturn is surrounded by rings. Although the rings look quite solid, they are actually bands of millions of pieces of ice and icy rock that are moving around Saturn. The rings are mainly brown and black in color.

19

What is a comet?

Comets are giant balls of ice and dust, like big, dirty snowballs. When comets come near the Sun, the ice melts, and tails of ice and dust form that look like fiery tails. The tail always points away from the Sun.

Do comets last forever?

Most comets last for thousands of years. Some comets, such as Halley's Comet, can be seen in the sky every 75 years or so. Sometimes bits of dust from the comet burn up and fall to Earth. This can look like a star falling down and is called a meteor, or shooting star.

1085   1535   1910

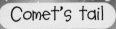
Comet's tail

? True or false

Rocks from space make huge holes in the Earth.

True. There are many holes (or craters, as they are called) around the world made by space rocks crashing to the ground. Most of these craters are quite small, but some are enormous. The biggest crater that we know of is in Africa.

↑ Showers of stars
Sometimes we see showers of shooting stars or just a single one. If you see a shooting star, you should make a wish!

When is a planet not a planet?

When it is Pluto! Pluto used to be called a planet, but scientists have now decided that it is a dwarf planet. Scientists have also discovered other dwarf planets that are even further from the Sun than Pluto.

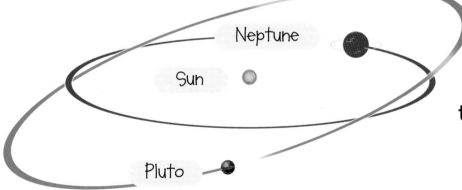

Neptune

Sun

Pluto

Can we see into space?

Yes, by using big dishes called radio dishes. Each dish collects radio waves from space. Scientists use these radio waves to build a picture of what is happening in space. A line of small dishes takes a better picture than one giant dish. Telescopes using mirrors also see pictures from space.

Radio dishes

What can I see from Earth?

Quite a lot! On a clear night, with not many clouds in the sky, you can see lots of stars. You can see more if you go to a place where there isn't much light from shopping malls and streetlights.

Can we take pictures in space?

Yes, the Hubble Space Telescope is a powerful telescope with a giant electronic camera.

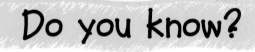

It takes better pictures of the stars and planets than telescopes on Earth because it is above the Earth's atmosphere.

Do you know?

1. Can we take pictures in space?
2. Where is the best place to look at the night sky?

Answers: 1. Yes, using special equipment. 2. A place where it is quite dark.

← Super sight

Looking through a telescope at the night sky makes the stars and planets look much clearer. Before telescopes were invented, we didn't know some planets existed.

Who goes into space?

Astronauts are people who travel into space. Astronauts go into space to do scientific research and repair spacecraft. Astronauts have also been into space to explore the Moon. In space, astronauts wear special suits to protect them from the cold and dangerous rays.

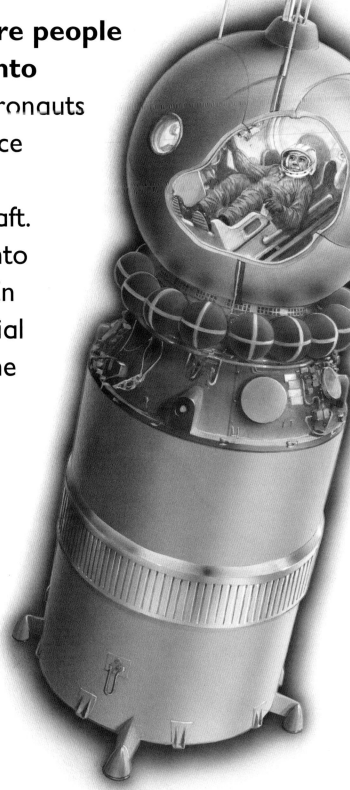

↑ First ape in space

Ham the chimpanzee was the first ape in space. The first animal in space was a dog called Laika. Since then, lots of animals have traveled to space.

Who landed on the Moon first?

Two men from America were the first to step on the Moon in July 1969. They were Neil Armstrong and Edwin "Buzz" Aldrin. Neil Armstrong stepped onto the Moon first, followed by Aldrin.

→ **Space games**
Astronauts have driven in a special buggy, taken photographs, and even played golf on the Moon!

Why do you weigh less on the Moon?

The Moon is smaller and lighter than Earth, so gravity is much weaker. On the Moon, you weigh about six times less than you do on Earth. Imagine how far and high you could jump!

? True or false

There are footprints and tire marks on the Moon.

True. There are astronaut footprints on the surface of the Moon. There are also tire marks made by the lunar rover, a special Moon buggy. There is no wind to blow the prints away.

Are shuttles like planes?

No, a space shuttle blasts off strapped to huge tanks full of rocket fuel. Once the shuttle's engines are running, two thin booster rockets give extra lift. These rockets then drop off and parachute into the sea. The fuel tank burns up in space. Minutes later, the shuttle is in orbit in space.

↑ Floating food

Weightlessness in space means food and drink float in the air. Liquid floats out of a cup and into the air, like a soap bubble. In space, you have to drink from a squeezy pack.

Fuel tank

Booster rockets

Space shuttle

Shuttle in orbit

Space station

A space station is a huge spacecraft that travels around the Earth. Scientists live, work, and do experiments there.

Space station

Shuttle falling back to Earth

Do you know?

1. Do people live in space?
2. Can a space shuttle take off like a plane?

Answers: 1. Yes, in space stations.   2. No, it is launched into space like a rocket.

What does a shuttle do?

It carries things into space. Shuttles take spare parts to space stations. They also repair satellites and carry astronauts to space stations. To get back to Earth, the shuttle slows down. It gets very hot when it falls to Earth, but special tiles keep it from burning.

27

Who lives in space?

Scientists live in space stations like this one. Living in space is strange because of the weightlessness—everything floats in the air. To go to sleep, you need to be strapped into bed. When you go to the bathroom you have to put everything in a bag to keep it from floating about.

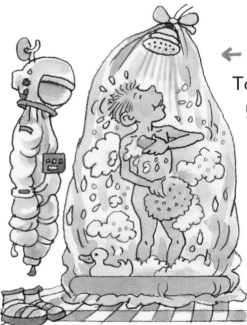

← Showering in space
To have a shower in space, you have to get inside a specially designed waterproof bag. If you were to use a normal sink or shower, the water would float all over the place.

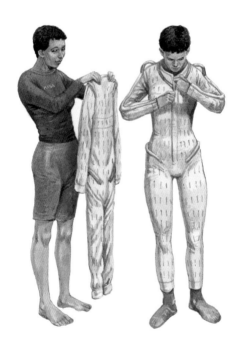

← Going solo

When astronauts go out into space, they sometimes have to wear a strap-on spacecraft to help them move around. This is like having an engine strapped to their back! They use controls to move in different directions.

What is a space suit?

Space suits are special clothes that keep astronauts alive. They wear them only when they leave the spacecraft. They give the astronauts air and protect them from rocks that may be whizzing about. It's very hot in the suit, so they wear cool clothes underneath. The helmet protects their eyes from the Sun.

Could we live in space?

We could not live on any other planet in the Solar System. We need air to breathe and plenty of water. But it might be possible to change a planet to make it more like home. This would mean living in big glass domes that have air and water piped into them.

← Meet the neighbors
There might be life on one of Jupiter's moons that is covered in ice. Under the ice, there might be warm water, where amazing water creatures might live.

Do aliens exist?

Many people think that beings could live on other planets deep in space. However, space is such a big place we might never find them! Or there might be life only on Earth.

Are there robots in space?

Yes, there are! We have sent many robot space probes into space to explore the planets. Some have finished their jobs and flown away into deep space. New robots are being launched into space every year to make exciting new discoveries.

Index

This edition updated and published in 2011
4 6 8 10 9 7 5
The Southwestern Company
Nashville, Tennessee
© Southwestern Company 2002, 2005, 2010

ISBN 978-0-07197 519 5

Miles
KeLLy

 Southwestern

Produced by Miles Kelly Publishing Ltd
Harding's Barn, Bardfield End Green, Thaxted, Essex,
CM6 3PX, UK

Publishing Director: Anne Marshall
Designer: Warris Kidwai
Assets: Lorraine King, Cathy Miles

Printed in China

Project Director, UK: Fiona Greenland
Editorial Director: Mary Cummings
Managing Editor: Judy Jackson
Copy Editor: Carolyn King
Production Manager: Powell Ropp

The publishers would like to thank the following artists whose work appears in this book: John Butler, Steve Caldwell,
Jim Channell, Andrew Clark, Mark Davis, Kuo Kang Chen, Andrew Clark, Peter Dennis, Heather Dickinson, Richard
Draper, James Field, Nicholas Forder, Chris Forsey, Mike Foster/Maltings Partnership, Terry Gabbey, Alan Hancocks,
Richard Hook, John James, Emma Jones, Tony Kenyon, Aziz Khan, Sue King/SGA, Kevin Maddison, Janos Marffy, Debbie
Meekcoms, Helen Parsley, Rachel Philips, Jane Pickering, Neil Reid, Terry Riley, Pete Roberts, Steve Roberts, Peter
Sarson, Martin Sanders, Mike Saunders, Sarah Smith, Studio Galante, Rudi Vizi, Mike White, Paul Williams, Peter Wilks.